Z 19107   11/92

Z 19107

HISTORIC

COMMUNITIES

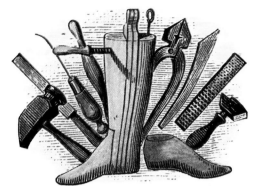

Colonial Crafts

Bobbie Kalman

Crabtree Publishing Company

HISTORIC
COMMUNITIES

Created by Bobbie Kalman

_____

For Julie Harder

_____

Illustrations
Antoinette "Cookie" DeBiasi

Research and Editing
Jodi Gaspich

Design and Mechanicals
Antoinette "Cookie" DeBiasi

Color Separations
ISCOA

Printer
Worzalla Publishing

Special thanks to: Cathy Grosfils, Laura Arnette, John Caramia, Art Werner, Renee Harsch, Amy Krupp, Melissa McCuen, Katie Root, Jaime Dimmig, and Stephen Wargo.

Published by
Crabtree Publishing Company

350 Fifth Avenue	6900 Kinsmen Court	73 Lime Walk
Suite 3308	P.O. Box 1000	Headington
New York	Niagara Falls, Ontario	Oxford OX3 7AD
N.Y. 10118	Canada L2E 7E7	United Kingdom

Cataloguing in Publication Data
Kalman, Bobbie, 1947-
    Colonial crafts

(Historic communities)
Includes index.
ISBN 0-86505-490-8 (bound) ISBN 0-86505-510-6 (pbk.)

1. Industrial Arts - History - 18th century - Juvenile literature.
2. Artisans - History - 18th century - Juvenile literature.
3. Frontier and pioneer life - Juvenile literature.
I. Title. II. Series: Kalman, Bobbie, 1947- . Historic communities.

TT18.K35 1992   j680'.9' 033

Contents

The craftspeople

In colonial times there were no factories. If someone needed a barrel or a chair, that object had to be made by hand. Craftspeople made furniture, utensils for the home, and tools for farmers. Each of these essential **artisans** was skilled in one particular craft. The wheelwright, for example, made wheels.

Craftspeople helped colonial towns grow. When several craftspeople opened shop, they attracted new settlers into the area. Visitors from other places also came to buy items sold at the shops of the artisans.

How did people pay?

Craftspeople sold their goods at their shops and charged customers the amount it cost to make a product, plus a small profit. Some customers were able to pay cash, but most left a note promising to pay later. Sometimes shopkeepers accepted farm produce such as eggs or flour in exchange for their goods or services. This exchange was known as **country pay** or the **barter system**.

Baskets were used for carrying and storing a wide variety of objects, so the basketmaker was a busy craftsperson. Cedar, ash, hickory, and white oak are examples of the kinds of wood used for making baskets. The wood was split again and again until the pieces were very thin. The long, flexible pieces of wood were then woven into baskets of different shapes and sizes.

Learning from others

The colonial craftspeople did not learn their skills by going to school. There were very few schools in those days, and only the sons of the rich could afford to attend them. Craftspeople learned their trades by working as **apprentices** to other craftspeople. Young boys and girls between the ages of ten and fifteen became apprentices.

An apprentice learned a trade on the job. The young boy in the picture is learning to use a drawknife. He is a carpenter apprentice.

Different jobs for boys and girls

Boys were apprenticed to craftsmen such as coopers, wheelwrights, and printers. If a father was a craftsman, his son usually learned his trade. Girls learned the domestic industries of spinning, weaving, sewing, and candlemaking. In those days girls seldom worked outside the home.

Long years of training

Apprentices served terms of between four and seven years. In the first year or two they performed simple tasks such as sweeping, running errands, and collecting payments. In the years that followed, apprentices learned to use the tools of their future trades.

Food, clothing, and a basic education

The master craftsman taught the apprentice all the skills, secrets, and talents of his craft. He called this knowledge his "mystery." Apprentices also learned how to read, write, and make simple arithmetic calculations, called **ciphering**. They were provided with clean clothes, shelter, and food. In return for their training, apprentices worked long hours without pay.

Creating a masterpiece

At the end of his or her term each young apprentice was required to produce a finished object. This piece of work was called a **masterpiece** because it was judged by the master craftsman. If the piece was well made, the apprentice passed his apprenticeship and became a **journeyman**. Journeymen traveled the countryside making and repairing goods until they saved enough money to open their own shops.

Apprentices started off doing simple jobs such as running errands and making deliveries.

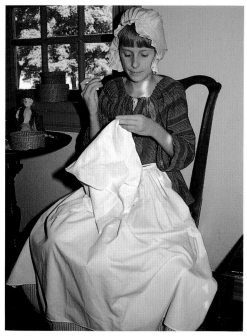

Girls were taught the domestic crafts of sewing, quilting, spinning, and weaving.

*The harnessmaker is making a **portmanteau**. It is a small bag in which clothes are rolled before they are packed.*

The leatherworkers

Leather was used to make many different items such as shoes, saddles, and harnesses. The two most common leatherworkers in the colonies were the harnessmaker and shoemaker.

The harnessmaker

The harnessmaker was a busy craftsperson. People depended on horses for work and travel, so they needed saddles and harnesses. Both were made from many pieces of leather, which were stitched together carefully. The leather used by the harness-maker was thick and heavy and came from large animals such as cows and buffalo.

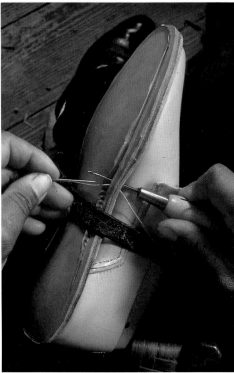

Tiny stitches were required to sew the soles of the shoes to the uppers.

The shoemaker

Shoemakers made shoes and boots. They could complete two pairs in one twelve-hour day. Before making shoes, the shoemaker had to carve a number of **lasts**. Lasts were foot-shaped blocks of wood whittled by hand in sizes small, medium, and large.

A leather **upper** was stretched over the last and fastened with glue until it was ready to be sewn to a sole. The sole was cut and pounded into shape with a hammer. Using an **awl**, the shoemaker made holes in the thick leather to allow waxed thread to pass through it. After the upper and sole were sewn together, the heel was attached with tiny nails. The finished shoes were polished with wax or oil.

Both shoes of a pair looked identical because making identical shoes was cheaper and simpler. People also liked the tracks that identical shoes left behind.

An apprentice was in charge of turning the wheel of the lathe, to which a belt was attached. The belt spun the object that was being shaped. Chair and cabinet legs were carved on the lathe. It took great skill to carve four identical legs.

In colonial times there were no banks, so many people kept their money and jewelry in their cabinet drawers. To protect small valuables, secret drawers were built in hidden panels. The carpenter in the picture is showing a drawer with a secret compartment.

The cabinetmaker

Cabinetmakers made beautiful furniture by hand. They also repaired musical instruments and constructed coffins. Since making coffins was part of the business of cabinetmaking, it was only natural that these artisans should also handle the funeral arrangements for the people in town. They even provided the hearses in which the coffins were carried!

Perfect joints

Cabinetmakers were sometimes called **joiners** because they were experts at joining pieces of wood. Perfectly fitted joints were strong, neat, and invisible to the eye. They were carved by hand and held together without glue or nails.

The big-wheel lathe

Cabinetmakers used hand tools made of wood and metal. Their biggest and most important tool was the **lathe**, a great wooden wheel that turned a piece of wood so the cabinetmaker could carve it into the desired shape. The legs of cabinets, chairs, tables, and beds were carved on the lathe.

The finishing touches

When a piece of furniture was completed, it was treated with **finishes** such as stains, vegetable dyes, oils, and varnishes. Cabinetmaker apprentices spent much of their time polishing and rubbing in these finishes. Sometimes **veneers** were used to decorate the tops of cabinets and tables. Veneers are thinly shaved sheets of wood that are glued in sections to the face of a cabinet. The grains of a veneer made beautiful patterns on tabletops and cabinet doors.

The cabinetmaker uses a drawknife to shave pieces from wood. It takes a long time and many shavings to get just the right shape.

*Making leakproof barrels was the cooper's art. Each barrel, bucket, and piggin was made from staves. The cooper in front is carving a stave on a shavinghorse. The man in the center is about to smooth one on a **jointer**. The rear cooper hammers an iron ring onto the finished barrel.*

The cooper

In the early days wooden pails and barrels were used to store both liquids and dry items. At one time a barrel was made by hollowing out a log. This was a very difficult task, so people were happy to have a cooper in town. Coopers made barrels, buckets, piggins, and pails.

The staves were cut with an ax. They were shaped wide in the middle and narrow at the ends.

Making the staves

Everything the cooper made was constructed with **staves**. Staves were wooden planks carved from pine, cedar, or oak. They were cut from large pieces of wood. The cooper shaped the staves wide in the middle and narrow at the ends so they would fit together to make a barrel. A **shavinghorse** held each stave in place as the cooper carved it.

Getting the barrel shape

When the staves were the right shape, they were placed side by side. A **trussing ring** held them upright in a circle. The staves were heated to make them bend and were then pulled together tightly using a rope and a crank, called a **windlass**. Several hoops were hammered onto the finished barrel to hold its shape and prevent the container from leaking.

Topping it off

The round lids for each barrel were cut from wide planks of wood. A **bunghole** was carved into the top lid. Liquids were poured in and out through the bunghole. A **spyhole** was bored into the middle of the barrel to allow people to see what the barrel contained. Plugs were carved to fit each bunghole and spyhole securely.

The wheelwrights in this picture are showing some of the stages of making a wheel. Which one is 1. shaping a hub on a lathe 2. carving a felloe 3. fitting tenons into a hub 4. joining felloes into a rim? Which wheelwright is called a turnwheel?

While ironing the tire, the wheelwright and two assistants worked quickly so the wooden wheel would not be set on fire by the hot iron hoop. Right after the hoop was hammered on, the wheelwrights threw water onto the wheel to cool the hoop. There was a lot of smoke and a loud hissing noise as the hoop suddenly tightened around the wheel. The hoop had to fit securely so that it would not fall off when the wheel was in motion.

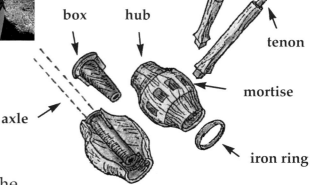

The wheelwright

The wheelwright made wheels for carriages, wagons, and carts. He started with the **hub**, the wheel's center. The hub was the strongest part of the wheel. It held a dozen or more spokes in place. The hub was made from the center core of a tree trunk that had been left to age for seven years. It had to be perfectly dry. Through its center ran the **axle**, a cast-iron tube on which the wheel turned. The rim of the wheel was made in seven or more curved sections, called **felloes**. The felloes were joined together to form a full circle.

*Both ends of the spokes were tapered to fit tightly into the hub and wheel rim. These carved ends were called **tenons**. The tenons fit into **mortises**, or holes, which were carved into the hub and felloes.*

Ironing the wheel

When the wheel was finished, an iron ring, called a **tire**, was added to its rim. It was heated and then hammered onto the wooden wheel. This process was called **ironing the wheel**. The tire was a bit smaller than the wheel so that it would fit securely. When heated, it expanded just enough to be placed around the wheel.

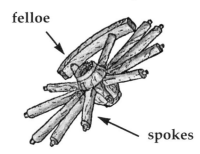

*A wheel was made of wood, but iron rings were added to its hub and rim to make them stronger. The hollow cone of iron inside the hub, called the **box**, held the **axle**, which joined the two wheels on opposite sides of the carriage.*

15

The wood from which the stock of the rifle was made was dried for three years before it was whittled into a rifle shape. Raised carvings added to its fine workmanship. Brass or silver ornaments decorated the finished rifle. Eighteenth-century guns were works of art!

The gunsmith

Long ago almost everyone owned a gun for hunting and protection. The gunsmith was always busy making and repairing these dangerous weapons. He worked with iron, steel, brass, silver, and wood.

A gun had three main parts: the **barrel**, **stock**, and **flintlock**. The barrel was a tube of iron in which the ammunition was placed. The stock was the wooden end of the gun. The flintlock was the device used to fire a rifle. When the trigger was pulled, a steel **frizzen** hit the flint and created sparks. The sparks caused some of the gunpowder to ignite, thereby resulting in the explosion of the rest of the powder. The explosion shot the ball from the gun.

To make the barrel, the gunsmith heated iron white hot, hammered it flat, and shaped it around a rod. The rod was then removed. The interior was bored out to make a straight tunnel. Spiral grooves were cut into the barrel chamber to make the rifle balls spin when fired. This helped the balls fire in a straight line.

17

The blacksmith

Iron was not an expensive metal, but it was very valuable to the early colonists. It was used to make important tools and equipment such as guns, nails, plows, pots, knives, padlocks, and horseshoes. People depended on the blacksmith to forge these necessary items. Most blacksmiths not only made horseshoes, they also shod horses and oxen. Because they knew animals well, they sometimes acted as veterinarians.

The forge was made of bricks with a bellows at one end and a hood, or hovel, at the other end. The bellows fanned the fire; the hovel carried smoke and fumes out through the chimney.

Many kinds of tongs and hammers were necessary to hold and shape the heated iron. Tongs were used to hold the red-hot metal in one hand so that it could be hammered and formed with the other hand.

The forge and anvil

The most important tool of the blacksmith was his coal fire, or **forge**. Without a fire a blacksmith could not make iron soft enough to bend. The blacksmith's **anvil** was a large, heavy, cast-iron tabletop with a cone at one end. Its surface was made of steel, which was harder than iron and could not be cut or damaged. The iron that was hammered and shaped on an anvil was called **wrought iron**.

Controlling the fire

The blacksmith controlled the heat of his fire using a **bellows**, **slice**, and **washer**. The bellows was a large leather bag that filled and emptied of air. When its cord or chain was pulled, the air inside was squeezed out and blown into the forge to make the fire hotter. When the cord was released, the bellows filled with air again. The slice was a long-handled rake that was used to spread out the coals in order to make the fire less hot. The washer was a bundle of twigs used to flick water on the fire to extinguish some of the coals. A tub of water stood nearby to cool, or quench, the hot iron.

The blacksmith used the sturdy anvil as a workbench on which he shaped his metal with a hammer.

*The slabs of iron that the blacksmith heated varied in temperature and color. Pieces of heated metal that were white, yellow, orange, red, or purple were handled in different ways. A blacksmith's trained eye could tell how hot and bendable, or **malleable**, a piece of metal was by its color.*

Where did the blacksmith get his name?

Can you guess how a blacksmith got his name? If you said he works with iron, which is a black metal, you are partly right. The word "smith" comes from the word "smite," which means "to hit or pound." A blacksmith, then, is a metal-worker who pounds black metal.

The founder

The founder melted different metals together to create new metals. This process was called **smelting**. Founders smelted: 1. copper and zinc to make brass; 2. copper and tin to make bronze; 3. tin, lead, and copper to make pewter.

The founder heated the metals in a heat-resistant graphite container called a **crucible**. Using tongs, he placed the crucible into the hot coals of the forge. It remained there until the metal it contained became **molten**. The liquid metal was poured into a mold through a small opening. This was a very dangerous job. Molten metals are scorching hot! When the metal hardened inside the mold, the finished piece was removed and joined with its other side.

(left) The founder's most challenging task was shaping the molds for casting metals. Molds were made inside iron frames called flasks. The founder packed fine sand into a flask and imprinted a pattern to make an impression in the sand. When the pattern was removed, its hollow image was left behind. Each side of an object was imprinted in a separate flask. (right) Much polishing and filing was needed to finish a candlestick.

The silversmith

Silversmiths worked with precious metals such as gold, silver, brass, and copper. They hammered these metals into objects and engraved delicate patterns on them. Silversmiths also melted and cast metals in molds, as the founder did.

In colonial times there were no banks in which people could put their silver coins. Instead of hiding the coins, people took them to a silversmith to be melted down into plates, spoons, and candlesticks, which were engraved so that people could identify them if they were stolen.

The silversmith's workbench could seat up to five people, allowing them all to work by the light of the window.

The papermaker, printer, and bookbinder

In the early days paper was made from linen rags. The rags were washed, cut up, and boiled in fresh water. Once the cloth broke into tiny pieces, the pulp that resulted was beaten into a thick batter. The pulp was strained through a sieve, formed into sheets of paper on a frame, and dried in presses.

The papermaker dipped a rectangular sieve into the pulp. The sieve was a piece of wire mesh stretched across a wooden frame. Another frame, called a deckle, was placed on top. The sieve and deckle were dipped into the pulp, raised up, and shaken gently back and forth. Water drained through the sieve. The deckle was removed, and the sieve was handed to the coucher, who dumped the newly formed sheet of paper onto a stack of felt. This step was called couching off.

The printer

Much of the paper made by the papermaker was used by the town printer who printed books, advertisements, and newspapers. The skilled printer composed type letter by letter and positioned it line by line on a page-sized tray, called a **galley**. The type in the galley was locked in place inside a frame called a **chase**.

The beater and puller

Two workers completed the printing process. They were called the **beater** and **puller**. Using a rocking motion, the beater spread ink across the type with leather ink balls. These balls soaked up the ink from a tray and released it onto the type.

A clean page was placed on a wooden frame, which folded down over the inked typeface. The puller then pulled an iron bar to lower the press plate down against the type, thereby pressing, or printing, the inked letters on the sheet of paper.

The beater spread ink across the typeface with leather ink balls.

The bookbinder

To **bind** a book is to sew and fasten it to a cover. Most books consist of a number of **signatures**. Each signature is a folded booklet that contains from four to sixteen pages.

The colonial bookbinder lined up all the signatures that made up one book one on top of the other with each of their folds, or **spines**, facing the same way. The signatures were then placed on a platform with their spines along the strings of a sewing frame. To join all the pages together, threads were sewn through the folds of the signatures and around each string.

A waxed linen thread was used to sew the signatures together. The thread fastened each string of the frame to the signatures.

Trimmed and bound

When completed, the book was released from the frame and the vertical strings were left to be sewn to cover boards. Next, the book was trimmed on a **trimming press**. After the pages were trimmed, the cover boards were fastened to the outer signatures and tied with the loose strings. A beautiful leather cover completed the binding.

The milliner

When an item of clothing could not be mended at home, it was taken to the milliner's shop. The milliner made alterations, sewed garments, and sold fashions that came from Europe. Hats, belts, gloves, feathers, tassels, buttons, buckles, and shoes were some of the other items that could be bought at the milliner's.

Milaner to milliner

Do you know why this shopkeeper was called a milliner? In the early days many fancy items such as hats, fine fabrics, and lace came from the Italian city of Milan. "Milaners" were originally the people who lived in Milan, but soon the people who imported and sold clothes also came to be known as "Milaners" or "milliners."

To attract people who walked by, the milliner displayed dolls dressed in the latest fashions in the shop windows. The clothes worn by the dolls were available inside the shop.

The wigmaker

Wigs were worn by those who could afford their expensive prices. Wealthy children as young as seven years old were fitted for wigs. In the early days of the colonies, large wigs were considered fashionable. The most expensive wigs were made from human hair. It was not uncommon for people to have their hair cut off to be woven into wigs. Cheaper wigs were made from horsehair or silk.

To keep them clean and neat, wigs needed to be powdered with fine sand or flour dust and then shaken and combed. The powder absorbed the oils that built up from the person's own hair underneath. People did not wash their hair very often in those days!

*The wigmaker measured the circumference of a person's head to make a **caul**, or net cap. Individual hairs were knotted to a strong silk thread. The threads that contained the attached hair were sewn to the caul beginning at the nape of the neck and ending at the crown.*

To cut planks from a log, two men operated a double-handled pit saw. The log that was to be sawed was placed on a platform. One man stood on top of the log. The other stood in a pit below. Each man took a turn pushing and pulling the saw in order to cut through the log. It was very hard work, and the man below ended up covered with sawdust!

The building trades

Carpenters, brickmakers, and shinglemakers were all craftsmen who worked in the building trades. These men made the bricks, planks, and roofing materials that were needed to construct homes and other types of structures.

Brickmaking

To make a brick, the brickmaker first constructed a mold. He then prepared the clay from which the bricks were made. The clay was rolled in sand before it was placed in the brick-shaped molds. The wooden mold was covered with sand to ensure that the clay would not stick to it. The bricks were shaped, dumped out of the molds, and dried in the hot sun for several weeks. When kilns were used to dry the bricks, the bricks were ready in just a few hours.

Sawing planks

Before carpenters could build a house, they needed to construct a sturdy frame. Thick, strong planks were used to support a building. In colonial times there were few sawmills, so the planks had to be cut by hand. They were carved from tree trunks. A **pit saw**, such as the one shown on the opposite page, was used to cut the planks.

The shinglemaker

The roofs of houses were covered with shingles. Shingles were made from cedar or cypress trees. They were fastened to the roof in rows. Each row overlapped the top of the row before it. Because the shingles were tapered, they fit snugly together, keeping the rain from dripping through the roof.

The brickmaker made bricks from clay, which was found in the soils of the land. Clay was mixed with water and needed to be stirred continuously. A **pugmill**, *powered by a horse, stirred the gooey clay.*

The bricks in this brickyard were dried in a kiln.

Shingles were tapered to fit snugly together, thereby preventing the roof from leaking.

Home industries

The domestic industries provided the colonials with food, clothing, and light. Cooking, baking, spinning, and weaving were very important jobs. Each of these jobs was carried out by hand. The colonials baked sweet pies from the berries they picked, made candles from leftover animal fat, and spun and wove clothing from wool taken right off a sheep's back. Even soap had to be made from scratch. Women worked from morning 'til night to finish these difficult tasks.

The colonials worked very hard to feed themselves. They had to butcher animals for meat, milk cows for milk and butter, and grow their own grain for bread. The ingredients they used were prepared by hand. Sometimes it took a whole day to cook a meal!

The clothing worn by the colonials was made from flax, sheep's wool, or cotton. Using carding paddles, the wool was carded to fluff the fibers. (bottom) After spinning, the yarn was woven into fabric on a loom. (top)

Colonial crafts in the classroom

The students of Hoover Elementary School in Kenmore, N.Y. turned their classroom into a model of the colonial town of Williamsburg. They constructed streets and buildings, including several craft shops. They made reproductions of the craftspeople's tools and learned how these tools were used.

The students designed, cut, sawed, glued, constructed, and painted. They enjoyed their work and the unique learning experience.

The students built a blacksmith shop equipped with the tools of the blacksmith.

Glossary

ammunition Any explosive material such as gunpowder that is fired from a gun

apprentice One who is learning a trade under a skilled craftsperson

artisan One who is skilled in making special goods; a craftsperson

barter system The system of exchanging goods or services without using money

caul A cap onto which hair is sewn for the purpose of making a wig

ciphering The act of making simple arithmetic calculations

colonial, colonist An inhabitant of a territory that is ruled by a distant country; a person who lives in a colony

eighteenth century The period in history from 1701-1800

finish A substance used to create a smooth surface on furniture

graphite A heat-resistant mineral

jointer A tool used by the cooper to shape pieces of wood

mallet A hammer with a round wooden head

mold A hollow container into which hot fluid material is poured, so that when the fluid cools and hardens, it will take on the shape of the container

molten metal Any metal that has been heated to become liquid

piggin A small wooden bucket with an extended arm for a handle

smelting The process of melting metals in order to separate or combine them with other metals

trade An occupation or craft

trussing ring A ring used by the cooper to hold staves in place

varnish An oil-based liquid used to give wood a smooth, shiny finish

Index

Acknowledgments

Illustrations and cover design: Antoinette DeBiasi
Cover art: John Mantha
Photographers: All photographs were taken at Colonial Williamsburg except pages. 6, 11, 19 (right)
Courtesy of the Colonial Williamsburg Foundation: Cover, title page, pages 4-5, 8 (bottom), 9 (top), 10 (top), 12, 14, 15, 16, 17, 19 (left), 20 (left), 21 (top), 22, 26, 27, 28, 28, 29

Peter Crabtree and Bobbie Kalman; pages 7, 8 (top), 9 (bottom), 10 (bottom), 13, 18, 19 (right), 20 (right), 21 (bottom), 23, 24, 25, 30 (top left)
Art Werner; 30 (bottom left and right), 31
Jim Bryant; 6, 11

1 2 3 4 5 6 7 8 9 0 Printed in U.S.A. 1 0 9 8 7 6 5 4 3 2